AMAZING ANIMALS OF THE WORLD ①

Volume 6

Marmoset, Common — Owl, Great Horned

GROLIER

an imprint of

SCHOLASTIC

Scholastic Library Publishing

www.scholastic.com/librarypublishing

First published 2008 by Grolier, an imprint of Scholastic Inc.

For information address the publisher: Grolier, Scholastic Library Publishing
90 Old Sherman Turnpike
Danbury, CT 06816

Printed and bound in the U.S.A.

Library of Congress Cataloging-in-Publication Data
Amazing animals of the world 1.
v. cm.
Contents: v. 1. Aardvark-bobcat — v. 2. Bobolink-cottonmouth — v. 3. Coyote-fish, Siamese fighting — v. 4. Fisher-hummingbird, ruby-throated — v. 5. Hyena, brown-mantis, praying — v. 6. Marmoset, common-owl, great horned — v. 7. Owl, pygmy-robin, American — v. 8. Sailfin, giant-spider, black widow — v. 9. Spider, garden-turtle, common musk — v. 10. Turtle, green sea-zebrafish.
Includes bibliographical references and index.
ISBN 0-7172-6225-1; 978-0-7172-6225-0 (set : alk. Paper) - ISBN 0-7172-6226-X; 978-0-7172-6226-7 (v. 1 : alk. paper) - ISBN 0-7172-6227-8; 978-0-7172-6227-4 (v. 2 : alk. paper) - ISBN 0-7172-6228-6; 978-0-7172-6228-1 (v. 3 : alk. paper) - ISBN 0-7172-6229-4; 978-7172-6229-8 (v. 4 : alk. paper) - ISBN 0-7172-6230-8; 978-7172-6230-4 (v. 5 : alk. paper) - ISBN 0-7172-6231-6; 978-0-7172-6231-1 (v. 6 : alk. paper) - ISBN 0-7172-6232-4; 978-0-7172-6232-8 (v. 7 : alk. paper) - ISBN 0-7172-6233-2; 978-0-7172-6233-5 (v. 8 : alk. paper) - ISBN 0-7172-6234-0; 978-0-7172-6234-2 (v. 9 : alk. paper) - ISBN 0-7172-6235-9; 978-0-7172-6235-9 (v. 10 : alk. paper)
1. Animals—Encyclopedias, Juvenile. I. Grolier Incorporated. II. Title: Amazing animals of the world one.
QL49.A453 2007
590.3—dc22
2007012982

About This Set

Amazing Animals of the World 1 brings you pictures of 400 exciting creatures, and important information about how and where they live.

Each page shows just one species, or individual type, of animal. They all fall into seven main categories, or groups, of animals (classes and phylums scientifically) identified on each page with an icon (picture)—amphibians, arthropods, birds, fish, mammals, other invertebrates, and reptiles. Short explanations of what these group names mean, and other terms used commonly in the set, appear in the Glossary.

Scientists use all kinds of groupings to help them sort out the thousands of types of animals that exist today and once wandered the earth (extinct species). *Kingdoms*, *classes*, *phylums*, *genus*, and *species* are among the key words here that are also explained in the Glossary.

Where animals live is important to know as well. Each of the species in this set lives in a particular place in the world, which you can see outlined on the map on each page. And in those places, the animals tend to favor a particular habitat—an environment the animal finds suitable for life—with food, shelter, and safety from predators that might eat it. There they also find ways to coexist with other animals in the area that might eat somewhat different food, use different homes, and so on.

Each of the main habitats is named on the page and given an icon, or picture, to help you envision it. The habitat names are further defined in the Glossary.

As well as being part of groups like species, animals fall into other categories that help us understand their lives or behavior. You will find these categories in the Glossary, where you will learn about carnivores, herbivores, and other types of animals.

And there is more information you might want about an animal—its size, diet, where it lives, and how it carries on its species—the way it creates its young. All these facts and more appear in the data boxes at the top of each page.

Finally, the set is arranged alphabetically by the most common name of the species. That puts most beetles, for example, together in a group so you can compare them easily.

But some animals' names are not so common, and they don't appear near others like them. For instance, the chamois is a kind of goat or antelope. To find animals that are similar—or to locate any species—look in the Index at the end of each book in the set. It lists all animals by their various names (you will find the Giant South American River Turtle under Turtle, Giant South American River, and also under its other name—Arrau). And you will find all birds, fish, and so on gathered under their broader groupings.

Similarly, smaller like groups appear in the Set Index as well—butterflies include swallowtails and blues, for example.

Table of Contents
Volume 6

Glossary

Amphibians—species usually born from eggs in water or wet places, which change (metamorphose) into land animals. Frogs and salamanders are typical. They breathe through their skin mainly and have no scales.

Arctic and Antarctic—icy, cold, dry areas at the ends of the globe that lack trees but are home to small plants that grow in thawed areas (tundra). Penguins and seals are common inhabitants.

Arthropods—animals with segmented bodies, hard outer skin, and jointed legs, such as spiders and crabs.

Birds—born from eggs, these creatures have wings and often can fly. Eagles, pigeons, and penguins are all birds, though penguins cannot fly through the air.

Carnivores—they are animals that eat other animals. Many species do eat each other sometimes, and a few eat dead animals. Lions kill their prey and eat it, while vultures clean up dead bodies of animals.

Cities, Towns, and Farms—places where people live and have built or used the land and share it with many species. Sometimes these animals live in human homes or just nearby.

Class—part, or division, of a phylum.

Deserts—dry, usually warm areas where animals often are more active on cooler nights or near water sources. Owls, scorpions, and jack rabbits are common in American deserts.

Endangered—some animals in this set are marked as endangered because it is possible they will become extinct soon.

Extinct—these species have died out completely for whatever reason.

Family—part of an order.

Fish—water animals (aquatic) that typically are born from eggs and breathe through gills. Trout and eels are fish, though whales and dolphins are not (they are mammals).

Forests and Mountains—places where evergreen (coniferous) and leaf-shedding (deciduous) trees are common, or that rise in elevation to make cool, separate habitats. Rain forests are different (see below).

Freshwater—lakes, rivers, and the like carry fresh water (unlike Oceans and Shores, where the water is salty). Fish and birds abound, as do insects, frogs, and mammals.

Genus—part of a family.

Grasslands—habitats with few trees and light rainfall. Grasslands often lie between forests and deserts, and they are home to birds, coyotes, antelope, and snakes, as well as many other kinds of animals.

Herbivores—these animals eat mainly plants. Typical are hoofed animals (ungulates) that are common on grasslands, such as antelope or deer. Domestic (nonwild) ones are cows and horses.

Hibernators—species that live in harsh areas with very cold winters slow down their functions then become inactive or dormant.

Invertebrates—animals that lack backbones or internal skeletons. Many, such as insects and shrimp, have hard outer coverings. Clams and worms are also invertebrates.

Kingdom—the largest division of species. All living things are classified in one of the five kingdoms: animals, plants, fungi, protists, and monerans.

Mammals—these creatures usually bear live young and feed them on milk from the mother. A few lay eggs (monotremes like the platypus) or nurse young in a pouch (marsupials like opossums and kangaroos).

Migrators—some species spend different seasons in different places, moving to where more food, warmth, or safety can be found. Birds often do this, sometimes over long distances, but other types of animals also move seasonally, including fish and mammals.

Oceans and Shores—seawater is salty, often deep, and huge. In it live many fish, invertebrates, and some mammals, such as whales and dolphins. On the shore, birds and other creatures often gather.

Order—part of a class.

Phylum—part of a kingdom.

Rain forests—here huge trees grow among many other plants helped by the warm, wet environment. Thousands of species of animals also live in these rich habitats.

Reptiles—these species have scales, have lungs to breathe, and lay eggs or give birth to live young. Dinosaurs are thought to have been reptiles, while today the class includes turtles, snakes, lizards, and crocodiles.

Scientific Name—the genus and species name of a creature in Latin. For instance, *Canis lupus* is the wolf. Scientific names avoid the confusion possible with common names in any one language or across languages.

Species—a group of the same type of living thing. Part of an order.

Subspecies—a variety but quite similar part of a species.

Territorial—many animals mark out and defend a patch of ground as their home area. Birds and mammals may call very small or very large spots their territories.

Vertebrates—animals with backbones and skeletons under their skins.

Common Marmoset
Callithrix jacchus

Length: 20 to 23 inches (including tail)
Weight: 10 to 13 ounces
Diet: fruits, flowers, tree sap, insects, spiders, bird eggs, and frogs

Number of Young: 1 or 2
Home: eastern South America
Order: primates
Family: marmosets, tamarins

 Rain Forests

 Mammals

 Endangered Animals

© STEPHAN BONNEAU / BIOS / PETER ARNOLD, INC.

Common marmosets are small monkeys with silky fur coats, long tails, and white tufts of fur on their ears. They spend their time in trees looking for tree sap, fruits, insects, bird eggs, and other things to eat. They are always alert and on the lookout for their enemies. These include wild cats, snakes, and birds of prey.

Common marmosets live in small family groups of up to 13 individuals. Normally, only one female in the group mates and breeds during a particular breeding season. Chemical changes take place in the other females that prevent them from reproducing. Scientists do not yet understand why this is so. A female is pregnant for about 140 days. She usually gives birth to twins. A baby common marmoset is completely dependent on its mother. But by the time it is two months old, the young monkey begins to catch food, play with other group members, and travel through the trees on its own.

Common marmosets live in the tropical rain forests of Brazil. Unfortunately, the amount of rain forest decreases each year. People cut down the forest to make room for farms, towns, roads, and other development. The destruction of the rain forests has endangered the animals. Perhaps they will be able to survive by adapting to new habitats people create for them. Some common marmosets now live in woods at the edge of the large Brazilian city of Rio de Janeiro.

American Marten
Martes americana

Length of Body: 14 to 18 inches
Length of Tail: 6 to 8 inches
Weight: 1⅓ to 2¾ pounds
Diet: small animals, eggs, fruits, and nuts

Number of Young: 1 to 4
Home: North America
Order: carnivores
Family: badgers, otters, skunks, weasels, and relatives

 Forests and Mountains

Mammals

The American marten is a weasel-like predator. It has beautiful fur and a thick, bushy tail. Its pelt, called "American sable," is made into expensive coats. Not surprisingly, fur trappers have greatly reduced the number of American marten. Hunters continue to trap this species. But laws now limit the number that may be killed each year. Its natural enemies include lynx, coyotes, owls, eagles, and fishers (a larger type of marten). When running for its life, the marten often escapes by diving into deep water.

The American marten is itself a fearsome hunter. It is most at home in fir, spruce, and pine trees. There it prowls for its favorite foods: squirrels, mice, and birds. In the heat of a chase, the marten is a reckless speedster. It crashes through the treetops. It races along narrow branches. It leaps from swinging limbs. The agile marten also dangles from thin branches to reach fruits, seeds, and bird eggs.

The American marten breeds in midsummer. Over a few days, a female may mate with several males. Her pups are born the following spring. They weigh just 1 ounce each. The newborn marten remain in the nest for about two months. During the first four months, the mother teaches them to hunt. She then leaves her family to find a new mate.

Eastern Meadowlark
Sturnella magna

Length: 8 to 11 inches
Wingspan: 13 to 17 inches
Diet: mainly insects and spiders; also grain and weed seeds

Number of Eggs: 3 to 7
Home: Canada south to northern South America
Order: perching birds
Family: buntings, finches

 Grasslands

 Birds

© RALPH REINHOLD / ANIMALS ANIMALS / EARTH SCENES

The eastern meadowlark is a gardener's helper. It eats grasshoppers, caterpillars (including hairy ones!), other insect pests, and large quantities of weed seeds. This chunky bird can often be seen perched on fence posts, utility poles, and telephone wires at the edges of fields. The male and female are almost identical in appearance. The meadowlark's back is streaked with brown. And its bright yellow breast is marked by a black bib. On the ground its streaked back blends into the surroundings. This helps to make the meadowlark nearly invisible to predators. Unlike most birds, meadowlarks do not run or hop—they walk.

The eastern meadowlark builds its nest on the ground under a clump of grass or in some other concealed place. The nest is made of dry stems and grass. And it is lined with horsehair, pine needles, and other soft materials. The female lays her eggs in the nest. Then she incubates them for about two weeks. During this time, she turns the eggs often—sometimes as frequently as five times an hour. Turning helps to keep the eggs uniformly warm. Both parents feed the baby birds.

Eastern meadowlarks that breed in Canada and the northern United States migrate southward for winter. They fly north again in April. They travel day and night until they reach their summer homes.

American Mink
Mustela vison

Length: 26 to 35 inches
Weight: 1½ to 3½ pounds
Diet: muskrats, other small mammals, fish, snakes, and frogs
Number of Young: 3 to 8

Home: North America
Order: carnivores
Family: badgers, otters, skunks, weasels, and relatives

Freshwater

Mammals

© JOE MCDONALD / CORBIS

American mink mate in the middle of winter. A male mink mates with several females before the snow melts. But he settles down and raises a family with just one of them. He and his mate may move into a muskrat burrow. (They eat the muskrat first.) Or they may occupy an abandoned beaver den. As a last resort, they will dig their own den. They do this on the bank of a swift-flowing stream. Their young are born in April and May.

Mink parents are fearsome hunters and good providers. They catch fish and kill muskrats and rabbits their own size. They will even raid a farmer's henhouse if food is needed. Whatever they hunt, mink always kill in the same manner. They make a quick bite to the neck. In the wild, American mink are chocolate brown and black. The chin and throat are spotted white. Mink raised on mink farms are bred in many colors, including tan and white. Mink do not make good pets. They are fierce little animals and must be handled carefully. They are bred for their beautiful fur, which is sewn into expensive coats.

Mink farms may raise 20,000 or more animals in long rows of attached cages. The mink rancher is a busy cook. A large herd of mink will eat 5 tons of fresh food a day!

8

Mockingbird
Mimus polyglottos

Length: 9 to 11 inches
Diet: insects, fruits, and berries
Number of Eggs: 3 to 6
Home: North Central, and South America

Order: perching birds
Family: starlings

 Cities, Towns, and Farms

 Birds

© STEVE KAUFMAN / CORBIS

On a trip through the countryside, a group of bird-watchers might hear the songs of a dozen birds. They might even be lucky enough to see all 12. But if they see only one bird, they will know immediately that it is a mockingbird. One meaning of the word *mock* is "to imitate." And the mockingbird is one of nature's greatest imitators. Ornithologists (bird experts) have recorded a mockingbird singing the songs of more than 30 different kinds of birds.

The mockingbird lives in North, Central, and South America. In the United States, mockingbirds live mostly in the south. But they range as far north as northern New England and Michigan. They make their homes in open fields, farms, gardens, and parks. They prefer places with ample supplies of insects, seeds, and wild fruit. They build their nests in bushes, small trees, and thickets. Both parents build the nest and feed the young. But only the female incubates the eggs.

Mockingbirds may sing a lot, but they are not very social. They never flock together. They prefer to live alone or in pairs. They are fierce defenders of their own territory. They have been known to attack animals and people who come too close. And if a mockingbird sees its own image when hopping by a shiny hubcap or tin can, it will even attack that!

Star-nosed Mole
Condylura cristata

Length of Body: 4 to 5 inches
Length of Tail: 3 inches
Weight: 1½ to 3 ounces
Diet: aquatic insects, worms, crustaceans, mollusks, and fish

Number of Young: 2 to 7
Home: northeastern United States and Canada
Order: shrews, hedgehogs, moles, and relatives
Family: desmans and moles

 Freshwater

 Mammals

© MICHAEL HABICHT / ANIMALS ANIMALS / EARTH SCENES

Eyes and ears are almost useless to an underground creature. The sense of touch, however, is all-important. So the moles of the world have evolved into bizarre-looking, earless creatures with pin-sized eyes and long, sensitive noses. Yet there is one species of mole that is even more fantastic-looking than the rest. The star-nosed mole sniffles through life with 22 wiggling tentacles at the end of it hairless snout.

The star-nosed mole uses its starburst of nose "fingers" to feel for underwater prey. The star-nosed mole is a skillful swimmer that catches its food along the bottom of ponds, streams, and lakes. In addition to using its tentacles to hunt, the mole uses them to plug its nostrils as it swims. In the same way, the mole can cover its nose to keep out dirt as it digs its tunnels. If you look at a mole's front paws, you will see that they are broad, sharp shoveling tools. Like other moles, the star-nosed species digs an elaborate network of tunnels just below the surface of the ground. Star-nosed moles are especially adapted for shoveling through wet, swampy soil. They are always found near a body of water or in a very wet meadow.

While other species of mole build solitary burrows, star-nosed moles often form small colonies. Though they do not mate for life, many couples stay together through the winter.

Banded Mongoose
Mungos mungo

Length of Body: about 16 inches
Length of Tail: about 8 inches
Weight: 2 to 3 pounds
Diet: insects, spiders, reptiles, and fruits

Number of Young: 3 to 5
Home: Africa
Order: carnivores
Family: civets, mongooses

 Grasslands

 Mammals

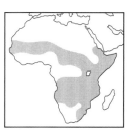

© ARON FRANKENTAL / GALLO IMAGES / CORBIS

Banded mongooses set out to hunt each morning. They do so in large, friendly groups of up to 20 family members. They roam across the African savanna. These busy creatures overturn rocks and dung heaps. They pull out roots and tufts of grass. And they stick their nose into burrows and other holes. Most of the day's food consists of insects and their larvae. But sometimes a group member finds a larger animal, such as a snake. Together, several mongooses attack the snake, kill it, and then share the meat. As they hunt, members of the group drift apart. They keep track of one another by constantly chattering as they work.

Members of this species look like all mongooses. They have a long body and tail, short legs, and a pointed face. The banded mongoose has white, tan, and brown stripes across its back. It is probably the friendliest of the mongooses, at least within its close social group. The entire group helps to raise the young.

Banded mongooses breed all year. Their mating is a very playful time. The male and female run in circles for an hour or more. After about eight weeks, the young are born in a deep lodge. This is often a dug-out termite nest. Playful and energetic, they grow quickly. They reach their adult weight in just six months.

Black Howler Monkey
Alouatta pigra

Length of Body: 22 to 36 inches
Length of Tail: 23 to 36 inches
Weight: 15 to 20 pounds
Diet: leaves and fruits

Number of Young: 1
Home: southern Central America
Order: primates
Family: New World monkeys

 Rain Forests

 Mammals

© THEO ALLOFS / CORBIS

Endangered Animals

Black howler monkeys are loudmouths! Each morning they wake up everyone in their jungle neighborhood. They are like rude alarm clocks. Their screams can be heard as far as 2 miles away. They scream again each afternoon. The noise starts with a soft growl. It then becomes a deafening racket.

A black howler's cry sounds like an army of giant killer monkeys. But howlers are very peaceful animals. Their families do not fight over territory. Instead, they just yell at one another from a distance. Black howlers are not very large. Most adults are less than 3 feet tall. So how do they make such a loud sound? Howlers have a special throat sac that inflates like a balloon. This sac is joined to a hollow bone. The bone acts like a microphone. It makes the howler's howl sound very loud.

The black howler is in danger of extinction in most of its range. This is because people are rapidly cutting down the jungle. But in Belize, villagers and monkeys have learned to live together. How have they done this? When the farmers clear land, they leave some trees for the black howlers. The villagers know they can earn money from the tourists who come to see the monkeys. And by not cutting down too many trees, the farmers do not overuse the land. They ensure that their children will have good soil for their crops. And the howlers will wake them up each morning!

Black Spider Monkey
Ateles paniscus

Length of Body: 15 to 25 inches
Length of Tail: 25 to 36 inches
Weight: 17 to 21 pounds
Diet: leaves, fruits, buds, and flowers

Number of Young: 1
Home: South America
Order: primates
Family: New World monkeys

  Rain Forests

Mammals

© TOM BRAKEFIELD / CORBIS

The black spider monkey is a wonderful acrobat. It swings from branch to branch and flies through the air in great leaps. Sometimes it even leaps backward! When it lands, it uses its long tail as an anchor. Wrapped around a branch, the tail has a grip so strong that a black spider monkey can safely dangle from the branch—perhaps to grab a juicy fruit or other snack.

The black spider monkey has glossy black fur, a white beard, and a light red face. It lives high in the treetops of tropical forests, seldom moving to the ground. But if it does, it is able to run along the forest floor.

Black spider monkeys live in groups. They are active during the day, when the social group breaks up into smaller groups of not more than 20 animals. Some of the groups may be made up of only males or females. The monkeys travel through the trees in search of food. If they spot danger, they let out a warning cry that sounds like a dog's bark. They also may break off tree branches and drop them at the enemy below.

The female black spider monkey gives birth to a single infant. During the infant's first few weeks of life, it is carried on the mother's belly as she travels through treetops. Later the baby travels on its mother's back. To keep from falling off, the youngster tightly coils its tail around its mother's tail.

Blue Monkey
Cercopithecus mitis

Length of Body: 1⅓ to 2¼ feet
Length of Tail: 2¼ to 3½ feet
Weight: 8¾ to 26½ pounds
Diet: fruits, green plants, flowers, and animals

Number of Young: 1
Home: central Africa
Order: primates
Family: Old World monkeys

Rain Forests

Mammals

© PETER JOHNSON / CORBIS

Blue monkeys get their name from the blue tint of their gray fur. However, not all are true to their name. Some blue monkeys are yellowish or reddish gray. All have a distinctive white crown, or "diadem," across the forehead. This marking gave rise to their less familiar name— diademed guenon.

The blue monkey is a relatively large, generally mellow creature. Yet it is often found in the company of smaller and livelier monkeys, such as redtails and colobi. These active little primates often lead the blue monkey to trees full of food. In return the large, intimidating blue monkey helps discourage predators from attacking its smaller cousins. To keep from fighting over food, the different species forage in slightly different places. Blue monkeys, for instance, may hunt for insects on the tree trunks. Redtails search for bugs in the leaves.

Despite its size, the blue monkey is very graceful in trees. It is most at home in very tall, dense jungle habitats. A typical blue monkey family has 10 to 40 members, but only 1 adult male. They live together in an area of between 25 and 175 acres. Rather than fight over territory, blue monkey troops chase away intruders by screaming loudly. It is the job of the head male to make the most noise. His booming call can carry for miles. Occasionally a bachelor blue monkey or an entire troop will ignore the warning calls. Then these normally peaceful monkeys attack fiercely.

Common Squirrel Monkey
Saimiri sciureus

Length: 10 to 14 inches
Weight: 1½ to 2½ pounds
Diet: fruits and insects
Number of Young: 1

Home: northern South America
Order: primates
Family: New World monkeys

  Rain Forests

 Mammals

© TOM BRAKEFIELD / CORBIS

Squirrel monkeys live in the forests of northern South America and the Amazon basin. They can be seen along riverbanks eating berries, seeds, flowers, leaves, and even insects or small animals. The squirrel monkey has a white face. Its mouth has a black ring around it, so it looks like a clown. It has a red coat and a long tail.

Squirrel monkeys form the largest troops of monkeys in South America. At night, their enemies, such as the ocelot and the puma, think twice before coming near groups of more than 100 little monkeys. Sometimes as many as 500 animals may gather. During the day, however, the large troop divides into several units to look for food. Squirrel monkeys talk to one another by making different sounds depending on their situation. They twitter when they meet. They bark at signs of danger. And they purr at mating time. After the birth of its young the female chases the male away. The newborn monkey settles on its mother's back for the first few weeks of its life.

The squirrel monkey is the most common monkey in South America. But it is still in danger. Monkeys are hunted and used for medical research. But these are not the worst dangers. More threatening still is the destruction of the Amazon forest by humans. Most squirrel monkeys live in this area. These creatures cannot survive if their home is destroyed.

De Brazza's Monkey
Cercopithecus neglectus

Height: 1½ to 2 feet (male); 1 to 1½ feet female
Weight: 1 to 18 pounds
Diet: fruits, leaves, and sprouts

Number of Young: 1
Home: central Africa
Order: primates
Family: Old World monkeys

 Rain Forests

 Mammals

© DANI / JESKE / ANIMALS ANIMALS / EARTH SCENES

The De Brazza's monkey can be found throughout central Africa. It lives mainly in treetops in moist forest regions. It also lives in mountain areas at altitudes of up to 2 miles. The monkey has a rounded head, dark olive gray fur, a white mustache, and a chin beard. It has a light orange red stripe on its forehead. This species of monkey has developed strong hind legs to launch itself into a leap. It uses its tail for balance.

The De Brazza's monkeys live in small groups. The groups include a single male, its mate, and their descendants. Within the groups, they observe a strict order. Babies, born seven to eight months after mating,

have pink faces and weigh almost 9 ounces. It is not known when the infants are weaned, nor is the life span of this species known. They come down from trees only in search of food. They eat mainly fruits, but also flowers, insects, and mushrooms. Their territories are small.

The De Brazza's monkey is a very quiet animal. It attracts little attention from possible predators. In fact, scientists are uncertain just what natural enemies the monkey has. What is known, however, is that when the monkeys sense danger, they stand motionless until the threat passes. Should the danger materialize, they emit a loud cry and flee for safety.

Night Monkey
Aotus trivirgatus

Length of Body: 11 to 19 inches
Length of Tail: 10 to 17 inches
Weight: 1½ to 2½ pounds
Diet: tender leaves, flowers, seeds, and insects

Number of Young: 1
Home: South America
Order: primates
Family: New World monkeys

 Rain Forests

 Mammals

© GREGORY G. DIMIJIAN / PHOTO RESEARCHERS

In all the world, only one species of monkey sleeps the day away. This creature, the night monkey of South America, comes out to hunt and play by the light of the moon. It sees quite well in the dim moonlight, thanks to its big, round eyes.

Night monkey families are small, and their members are very fond of one another. Biologists say that night monkey parents and offspring seldom fight. Once they have mated, the parents stay together for life. They bear just one baby at a time. However, an older child may stay with the family even after a younger brother or sister is born.

Night monkeys don't generally socialize outside their immediate families until it is time for a young adult to find its own mate. Sometimes, however, a popular fruit tree may be filled with more than a dozen night monkeys. On close examination, you would see that these are actually several small families, each keeping to its own branch. During the day, parents and offspring cozy up together in a hollow tree or leafy branch some 20 to 90 feet above the rain forest floor. As the evening falls, they awaken—stretching and yawning. One parent then scampers from the sleeping tree to a nearby fruit tree. If all is safe, the other parent follows and, finally, so do their offspring. In this way the family travels from tree to tree—until the morning finds everyone back in bed, cuddled together in a furry ball.

Proboscis Monkey

Nasalis larvatus

Length: 2½ feet
Weight: 15 to 44 pounds
Number of Young: usually 1
Diet: leaves, fruits, and flowers

Home: Indonesia and Borneo
Order: primates
Family: Old World monkeys

  Rain Forests

Mammals

Endang
Anima

© SUPRI / REUTERS / CORBIS

The proboscis monkey is named for the long nose that males of the species develop at maturity—about age seven. The male's nose may grow so long that it droops over his mouth. He may actually have to push it aside when he eats! The female proboscis monkey has a shorter, snubbed nose. The nose of the young proboscis curls upward, a little like a pert human nose.

Proboscis monkeys depend on mangrove trees for shelter. During the day, large troops of these monkeys rest together among the tree limbs. But at night, each adult sleeps alone on his or her own tree or branch. Unlike most primates, proboscis monkeys are good swimmers. Sometimes an entire troop will jump into the water to escape an enemy. When frightened by a boat, swimming proboscis monkeys can even dive underwater and hold their breath for 30 seconds or so.

In Borneo, this monkey is sometimes kept as a pet. But it is very difficult for zookeepers to keep this species alive outside its native home. They require a very special diet of swamp plants and bitter tropical fruits found only in their habitat. The proboscis monkey is now in danger of extinction. Modern technology has allowed humans to drain the mangrove swamps so crucial to the monkey's survival. And native people continue to hunt the proboscis monkey for its meat, which is considered a delicacy.

Rhesus Monkey
Macaca mulatta

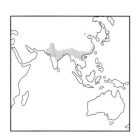

Height: about 2 feet
Length of Tail: about 13 inches
Weight: up to 26 pounds
Diet: mostly fruits, seeds, and other plant matter

Number of Young: 1
Home: Asia, from Afghanistan to China
Order: primates
Family: Old World monkeys

 Forests and Mountains

 Mammals

© ROBERT MAIER / ANIMALS ANIMALS / EARTH SCENES

The rhesus monkey shares important similarities with humans. So these animals are important for scientific research. Scientists used rhesus monkeys to develop various vaccines. Rhesus monkeys helped scientists test the polio vaccine. The rhesus monkey lent the first two letters of its name to the Rh factor. The Rh factor is a protein substance. It is found in human red blood cells. It was first discovered in the blood of the rhesus monkey. But most people know the rhesus as a friendly monkey that performs tricks. It is usually seen in circuses and carnivals. It is a popular animal in zoos.

In the wild the rhesus monkey lives in groups. About 10 to 100 individuals live in a group. A group usually has 8 adult females, 4 adult males, and their young. The group members groom one another. They rid one another's fur of insects and pests. Grooming may also help the monkeys to relax.

The rhesus monkey likes to climb trees. It also feels comfortable on the ground. It ranges into cities and towns. The rhesus is a sacred animal to the Hindu people of India. They try to protect and feed it. Other people consider it a pest. The rhesus steals food from gardens and orchards. The monkey stuffs food into its large cheeks. Then it scampers off for a private feast!

Moose
Alces alces

Length: 6¾ to 9 feet
Height at Shoulder: 6 to 7 feet
Weight: 900 to 1,400 pounds (male); 700 to 1,100 pounds (female)
Number of Young: 1 to 2
Diet: willows, woody plants, and aquatic vegetation

Home: North America, Europe, and Asia
Order: even-toed hoofed mammals
Family: deer, moose, and caribou

Forests and Mountains

Mammals

© ROBERT Y. ONO / CORBIS

The moose is the largest deer in the world. It is known as the elk in northern Europe. A moose has dark-brown hair and large ears. It has a stubby tail, a big muzzle, and huge antlers. Although quite large, moose can run very fast. A moose can race silently through forests at speeds of 35 miles per hour. They are also good swimmers. Moose can tread water at 6 miles per hour for two hours at a time. Moose live in spruce forests, swamps, and willow thickets. Their population has grown rapidly in recent years.

Moose are dangerous animals. They are very unpredictable. Moose avoid humans. But they will charge people, horses, or cars when provoked. Males thrash brush with their antlers to mark their territory. They occasionally fight violently over females. Usually, one male will withdraw. If their antlers lock, both moose could die. During the blackfly season, moose roll in mud. The mud protects them from the insects.

Mating season begins in mid-September. Males do not gather lots of females. They stay with one female for about a week. Then they move on to another. One or two calves are born eight months later. The calves are a dull reddish brown color. They can swim within two weeks. They are weaned after six months. Their mother drives them off just before the birth of the next new calf. A moose lives for about 20 years.

California Moray
Gymnothorax mordax

Length: up to 5 feet
Diet: fish
Method of Reproduction: egg layer

Home: coastal waters of southern California
Order: eels
Family: moray eels, morays

 Oceans and Shores

 Fish

© ROYALTY-FREE / CORBIS

The California moray is a brown green eel that lives in the warm waters off the coast of southern California and Mexico. This snakelike fish is common in areas where there are submerged rocks or coral reefs. During the day, it attaches the rear part of its long body to a reef or rock and waits for fish to come by. It grabs the fish with its powerful jaws and sharp, fanglike teeth. At night the California moray goes hunting for food. Like a snake, it slithers through the rocks and coral, searching for fish using its keen senses of smell and touch. The bite of the California moray is not poisonous, but the fish can inflict harmful wounds if provoked.

The California moray's skin is thick and leathery. Unlike most other fish, morays do not have scales. Nor do they have pectoral or pelvic fins. When they swim through the water, their motions are more like those of a snake than a fish.

When young morays hatch from their eggs, they look nothing like eels. They are so thin that they seem transparent. But, just as tadpoles turn into frogs, the moray larvae eventually turn into eels.

There are more than 100 kinds of moray eels. They were bred for food 2,000 years ago in ancient Rome. In many parts of the world, they are still considered a delicacy.

Mosquito
Culex sp.

Length: 3/16 inch
Wingspan: 3/8 inch
Rate of Wingbeats: 250 to 500 per second
Diet: blood, nectar, and sap
Method of Reproduction: egg layer

Home: worldwide
Order: gnats, mosquitoes, true flies
Family: mosquitoes

 Freshwater

 Arthropods

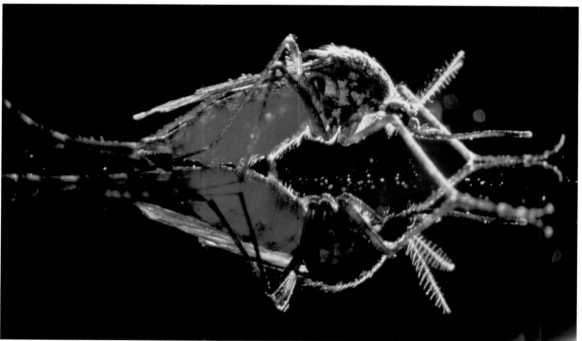

© ELISABETH SAUER / ZEFA / CORBIS

All mosquitoes have long needlelike tools on their mouths. They use them for sucking. But male mosquitoes never suck blood. They use their beaks only to drink food. They sip nectar from flowers and sap from plant stems. Females drink plant food, too. But most female mosquitoes need to drink blood. The blood helps the females to lay eggs. It provides the eggs with nourishing yolk.

The female mosquito lays her eggs in fresh water. She lays them on the surface in clumps. These clumps are called rafts. She places each egg in an upright position. She uses a sticky goo to fasten the eggs together. The newly hatched mosquitoes are called larvae. They are long and thin. They do not have legs. The larvae live in the water. They breathe air through tubes in their tails. The tubes run up to the water's surface. The larvae eat with pairs of brush-like hairs. They use them to pull water into their mouths. Inside their mouths the larvae have screens. These screens trap tiny floating plants and animals. Before young mosquitoes turn into adults, they change into pupae. They stop eating. Their bodies are enclosed in a shell. Then they grow new, adult bodies within the shells of their old bodies.

In temperate areas, mosquitoes are considered a nuisance. But in warmer climates, they are more dangerous. Their bites can be quite harmful to humans. Some tropical mosquitoes transmit serious diseases such as yellow fever and malaria.

Atlas Moth
Attacus atlas

Wingspan: 6 to 12 inches
Diet: leaves of trees and shrubs
Method of Reproduction: egg layer

Home: southeastern Asia and Indonesia
Order: butterflies, moths
Family: giant silkworm moths, royal moths

  Rain Forests

 Arthropods

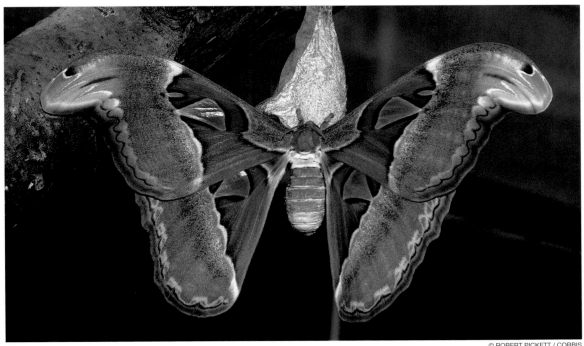

© ROBERT PICKETT / CORBIS

The Atlas moth is surprisingly beautiful. Its wings are covered with scales—like all moths and butterflies. The scales are shades of gold, brown, pink, gray, black, and red. There is a kind of transparent window at the center of each wing. Here there are no scales. You can see through the wings as through a real window. In front, the wings end with a point in the shape of a sickle. This point is lighter than the rest of the body. It has a dark spot and brown lines. It makes you think of a snake's head. What happens when a moth is disturbed? It extends its wings and lightly moves them. It then makes a little noise that attracts the attention of the disturber. When it sees what seems to be the head of a snake, it runs or flies away.

The caterpillar of the Atlas moth is huge. It can grow to be more than 4 inches long. It is green with darker rings. And it has a row of long spines on its back. It eats tropical tree leaves.

After two or three months, the caterpillar weaves a large cocoon and becomes a pupa. The cocoon sometimes weighs more than half an ounce. This is heavy compared with cocoons of other moths. It is very strong. People have tried to use this silk. But it does not have the quality of that from the silkworm moth. Because of its size and beauty, the Atlas moth is in great demand by collectors. This is why it is becoming very rare.

Gypsy Moth
Porthetria dispar

Wingspan: 2½ inches (female); 1 inch (male)
Diet: tree leaves
Method of Reproduction: egg layer

Home: native to Europe and Asia; introduced into North America
Order: butterflies, moths
Family: tussock moths

Forests and Mountains

Arthropods

© DARWIN DALE / PHOTO RESEARCHERS

Leopold Trouvelot thought he had a wonderful idea when he decided to start a silk industry in the United States. He imported some silk-producing caterpillars from Europe. But he soon abandoned the project. What happened? Unfortunately, by 1868 some of the gypsy moth caterpillars escaped into woods in Massachusetts. Lacking natural enemies, the gypsy moths quickly expanded their range and became serious pests on trees. Trouvelot's "wonderful idea" turned out to be a disaster.

Female gypsy moths are so heavy that they can barely fly. The smaller males fly about looking for the females, who give off a chemical odor that attracts the males. After mating, a female lays a mass of up to 1,000 eggs. The moths then die, after living less than two weeks as adults. The eggs hatch the following spring. The tiny caterpillars are the gypsies that give this insect its common name. They climb to the tops of trees and drop off on silken threads produced by glands in their abdomen. Wind carries them to a new location. Then they begin eating tree leaves. Gypsy moth caterpillars can devastate acres of trees. At times during summer, the caterpillars eat so much foliage that the trees are totally bare. They look much like they do in the dead of winter. In late June the caterpillars are about 2 inches long. They stop eating. Each caterpillar spins a cocoon around itself. During the next two weeks it metamorphoses, changing into an adult moth.

Luna Moth
Actias luna

Length of Adult: 7/8 to 1 1/4 inches

Length of Caterpillar: 2 3/4 inches

Diet: leaves of walnuts, hickories, and other trees

Method of Reproduction: egg layer

Home: eastern North America

Order: butterflies, moths

Family: giant silkworm moths, royal moths

 Forests and Mountains

 Arthropods

© GARY BRAASCH / CORBIS

The luna moth is not rare. But it is seldom seen, because it prefers forests to cities. The best way to find one of these large, velvety moths is to take a nighttime stroll along a rural, wooded road. You may find a moth resting in the light of a porch lamp.

Adult luna moths emerge from their cocoons in spring and immediately begin to search for mates. These moths do not eat. They live off the energy they stored as hungry young caterpillars. Female lunas lay their eggs in June, placing them in small clusters on the leaves of walnut and hickory trees. The adult moths die soon after the eggs are laid. Three weeks later the eggs hatch. As soon as the caterpillars emerge, they begin eating and growing at a furious speed. During the next eight weeks, they outgrow their skins—shedding and growing new ones—five times.

By the end of August, the caterpillars have grown to their full size and are ready to turn into adult lunas. Each caterpillar crawls onto a leaf and begins to spin a fine thread from its silk glands. They cover themselves with a thin, silky cocoon, which soon turns papery. When the leaves fall in autumn, the cocoons drop with them and are buried in the leaf litter that covers the forest floor through the winter. During this time the caterpillars inside their cocoons grow wings and adult moth bodies. When spring arrives, the lunas break out of their cocoons and fly off to find their mates.

House Mouse
Mus musculus

Length of Body: 2½ to 4 inches

Length of Tail: 2 to 3¾ inches

Weight: less than 1 ounce

Diet: mainly seeds

Number of Young: 3 to 16

Home: native to Asia; introduced throughout the world

Order: rodents

Family: mice, rats

 Cities, Towns, and Farms

 Mammals

© KEN WILSON / PAPILIO / CORBIS

House mice are cute and furry. But they are pests! They eat corn and other crops. They feed on foods in people's homes. They even gnaw on furniture, fabrics, and books. Sometimes they start fires. They do this by chewing through electrical wires. House mice also can make people sick. They carry the germs that cause typhus, spotted fever, and other diseases. But some house mice are very useful to people. White mice are a type of house mouse. Scientists use them in research laboratories.

House mice are very adaptable creatures. They are found in buildings all over the world. But they also live outdoors in many kinds of habitats. They live in fields, near woods, and on mountains. They are found at the edges of deserts. And they dwell in sugarcane plantations. The first house mice in North America arrived in the 1500s. They came aboard the ships of Spanish explorers.

House mice have keen senses of smell and hearing. These senses help mice find food. And they warn them if owls, hawks, cats, foxes, and other predators are nearby.

House mice can multiply rapidly if food is plentiful. A female mouse can have six litters a year. Each litter may contain a dozen or more babies. A baby mouse grows quickly. When it is two or three months old, it can have babies of its own.

Muskox
Ovibos moschatus

Length: 6½ to 8 feet
Weight: 400 to 800 pounds
Diet: grasses, sedge, flowering plants, and bushes
Number of Young: 1
Home: Canada, Greenland, and polar islands; introduced to Alaska and Norway

Order: even-toed hoofed mammals
Family: antelope, bison, buffalo, cattle, goats, and sheep

 Arctic and Antarctic

 Mammals

© KENNAN WARD / CORBIS

The sturdy muskox of the Arctic keeps warm under a double-layered coat of thick, fine wool and long, shaggy hair. Even its short tail and wide hooves are cozily encased in fur. In midsummer the wool undercoat falls out in huge clumps. This leaves the animal looking quite ragged until fall.

Summer is also the time when the male oxen battle for possession of their herds. The sparring can be dramatic. The bulls run at each other, head-on, from a great distance apart. Fortunately, their frightening crash is cushioned by the oxen's thick horns and skull. As part of a typical fight, each male marks the ground with a smelly "musk."

This is a secretion from glands above his eyes.

The muskoxen's natural enemies are the polar bear and the Arctic wolf. When attacked, a herd of muskoxen forms a circle. Their heads face outward, and their horns are lowered. Young calves stand in the middle of this fortress, well protected by their elders. This works well against wild animals. But human hunters can easily slaughter a circle of muskoxen. As a result, the muskox was nearly exterminated at the end of the 19th century. Since that time, however, the government of Canada has protected the animals. Their herds have slowly recovered.

Muskrat
Ondatra zibethicus

Length of Body: 10 to 14 inches
Length of Tail: 8 to 10 inches
Weight: up to 4 pounds
Diet: aquatic plants, frogs, and fish

Number of Young: 1 to 3
Home: North America, Europe, and Asia
Order: rodents
Family: mice, rats

Freshwater

Mammals

© JOHN CANCALOSI / PETER ARNOLD, INC.

Muskrats are aquatic rodents. They generally live in marshes, ponds, and quiet streams. They move awkwardly on land. But muskrats are excellent swimmers and divers. Their large, partially webbed feet and flattened, rudder-like tail help them. When it senses danger, a muskrat dives deep into the water. It can remain submerged for up to 20 minutes.

Most muskrats move about in the evening. They feed mainly on plants that grow near the water. Sometimes they venture into nearby fields to eat corn and other crops. Occasionally they also eat small aquatic animals. The muskrat's enemies include hawks, owls, mink, foxes, and otters. But people are its worst enemy. They

trap and kill muskrats for their brown fur. The animals are also prized for their musk, a secretion from musk glands. It is used for making perfume.

A muskrat burrows into a muddy bank or builds a lodge of reeds and grasses above the waterline. Both kinds of homes have underwater entrances. The animals mate during the spring and summer. A female muskrat has several litters each year.

The muskrat is a native of North America. It was introduced into Europe in 1905 for its fur. Since that time the species has spread throughout much of Europe and across northern Asia. In many places, it is considered to be a pest. Its burrows can damage dikes and dams.

Zebra Mussel
Dreissena polymorpha

Length: 1 inch
Weight: ¼ ounce
Diet: plankton
Number of Young: 400
Home: Europe and North America

Order: zebra mussels and relatives
Family: zebra mussels

  Freshwater

Other Invertebrates

© ED RESCHKE / PETER ARNOLD, INC.

Many animals in the world are endangered or threatened with extinction. But not the zebra mussel! In fact, the population of zebra mussels is growing. Unfortunately, its rising numbers are causing great problems for humans.

At one time, zebra mussels lived only in the ocean. Scientists think that long ago, a few attached themselves to the hull of a ship. They hitched a ride up a European river. Zebra mussels do not mind fresh water. And since one female can produce 400 offspring a year, they quickly spread all over Europe. In 1988 researchers discovered that they had also spread to North America.

Zebra mussels can cause big problems! One of the biggest problems is that they find their way into water pipes. They attach themselves to the inside surface of the pipes and begin reproducing. Soon the pipes are completely clogged. To make matters worse, the mussels are very hard to remove. They anchor themselves with extremely strong, gluey threads.

In large numbers, zebra mussels can empty a lake or reservoir of all other life. The zebra mussel feeds by pulling water through its gills and filtering out one-celled plants. These one-celled plants are call phytoplankton. A single zebra mussel can filter a quart of water a day. Soon there are no phytoplankton left for other small animals. And with no small animals to eat, larger fish and animals disappear as well.

Nightingale
Luscinia megarhynchos

Length: 6 inches
Diet: insects and berries
Number of Eggs: 4 or 5
Home: *Summer:* Europe
    Winter: Africa

Order: perching birds
Family: Old World flycatchers

 Forests and Mountains

 Birds

© ROGER TIDMAN / CORBIS

When it's not singing, the nightingale is difficult to locate and seldom noticed. It lives hidden in thick bushes, dense thickets, and wooded areas. It prefers areas near rivers or ponds. It nests in Europe, western Asia, and northwestern Africa. And it spends winters in Africa, south of the Sahara desert.

Most of a nightingale's life is spent on or near the ground. The male shares a rather small area with his mate. He does not allow any other nightingale near. The nightingale flies very little. It usually does so only when it has to chase invaders out of its territory. It has a slender body and strong legs. It moves in quick hops and looks for food in dead leaves and other waste. Often perched on a low branch, it leans over to catch its prey. Its preferred foods are small insects, butterflies, caterpillars, ant eggs, and larvae of all kinds. In September it eats a few berries as well.

You can hear the song of the nightingale only from mid-April to mid-June. It is certainly one of the most beautiful bird songs. The nightingale sings at night as well as in the daytime. Its night song seems more remarkable because the noises of the day have died down. On a still night, you can hear the nightingale's song from 1,500 to 2,500 feet away! The nightingale doesn't fly much during the summer. But it leaves Europe at the end of the warm weather. Its strong wings can take it to central Africa. There it spends the winter in milder conditions.

Common Wood Nymph
Cercyonis pegala

Wingspan: 2 to 2¾ inches
Diet: grass
Method of Reproduction: egg layer

Home: North America
Order: butterflies, moths
Family: satyrs, wood nymphs

 Cities, Towns, and Farms

 Arthropods

© WILD & NATURAL / ANIMALS ANIMALS / EARTH SCENES

Butterfly lovers never tire of seeing the lovely common wood nymph. These creatures flutter among the oaks and pines that grow along the roadsides and in the meadows and fields of North America. When a wood nymph lands on a tree to rest or drink sap, its dark brown wings blend so well with the bark that it becomes nearly invisible. Only when the butterfly flies off can you see the broad yellow bands on its front wings. Both sets of wings also carry pronounced "eyespots." These are yellow-rimmed circles surrounding a white or blue "pupil." The female wood nymph grows to a larger size and sports bigger eyespots than does the male.

Wood nymphs reproduce during the summer. They lay yellow eggs that have a distinctive key shape. Pale, grass green caterpillars emerge. These have four yellow stripes among their fine, fuzzy hair, and two reddish-colored tails. The caterpillars feed on various types of grass. They enter into hibernation soon after hatching.

Many varieties of wood nymph occur in North America. They are distinguished primarily by their eating habits. In the western United States and Canada, the butterfly often pollinates alfalfa and spirea. In the east the wood nymph prefers to eat rotting fruit. Despite their different diets, however, all the various wood nymphs are considered a single species.

Ocelot
Leopardus pardalis

Length: 2 to 3¼ feet
Height: 1⅝ feet
Weight: 24 to 35 pounds
Diet: small mammals, birds, and some reptiles

Number of Young: 2 to 4
Home: Central and South America
Order: carnivores
Family: cats

 Rain Forests

 Mammals

© FRANS LANTING / CORBIS

Endange
Anima

The ocelot is larger than a domestic cat. It has a dark yellow coat with brown spots or stripes. Its stomach is white, its shoulders have a swirl of hair, and its tail has brown rings or bands. No two ocelots have the same design on their coats. That is why their fur has been so valuable. Today, the ocelot is protected. The sale of its fur is against the law in most countries.

The ocelot lives in Central and South America. It mostly inhabits tropical forests, brushwood, and rocky regions. The life and habits of this beautiful animal are not well known because it is active only at night. It spends its day sleeping in a tree. At nightfall, it comes down from the tree and begins to hunt for prey. Most of all, it likes rodents, guinea pigs, agoutis (a kind of guinea pig), and porcupines. But it also eats hares and small deer, as well as birds and some reptiles. Like the fox, it steals poultry from farms. According to farmers, it even steals small calves.

The ocelot does not settle in one place. Rather, it marks its hunting territory with small piles of its excrement. Ocelots live in pairs. The male and the female hunt together and help each other capture game. They keep in contact by sending repeated calls. Mating takes place at night. It starts with howls similar to those of domestic cats, only louder. After two and a half months, two to four young are born. The birth occurs on a bed of leaves and grass, in the hollow of a tree, or in the middle of high rocks.

Common Octopus
Octopus vulgaris

Length: 2 to 10 feet
Weight: up to 55 pounds
Diet: crayfish, crabs, and other shelled animals
Number of Eggs: up to 150,000

Home: warm ocean waters worldwide
Order: octopuses
Family: octopuses

  Oceans and Shores

Other Invertebrates

© REINHARD DISCHERL / BIOS / PETER ARNOLD, INC.

The common octopus roams about on the ocean floor. It prefers the warm, shallow waters near the coast. It waits there until an unsuspecting sea creature happens by. Then, with eight arms for its use, the octopus tries to grab the prey. If the animal puts up a fight, the octopus squirts a cloud of black liquid (ink). The ink distracts the animal for a while. This gives the octopus time to catch the prey once more and perhaps bite the animal with its hard beak. Finally, the octopus puts the prey out of its misery. It quickly injects poison from a salivary gland.

The octopus's natural enemies are the conger eel and the shark. If the octopus is threatened by either of these, it might again discharge ink. The ink contains chemicals that reduce the attacker's sense of smell. This makes it more difficult for predators to follow the octopus after the ink has cleared.

The common octopus has many other remarkable features. Its eyes are similar to those of animals with backbones (vertebrates). One of the male's eight arms fertilizes the female. The female, in turn, cares for her eggs. She circulates water about them, cleans them, and attends to them until they hatch. The common octopus has a highly developed brain and nervous system. And it seems to have a capacity for learning.

Giant Pacific Octopus
Enteroctopus dofleini

Length of Body: 18 inches
Armspread: 15 to 32 feet
Weight: 40 to 100 pounds
Diet: small fish and
  crustaceans

Number of Eggs: about
  150,000
Home: north Pacific Ocean
Order: octopuses
Family: octopuses

  Oceans and Shores

Other Invertebrates

© JEFFREY ROTMAN / CORBIS

The Pacific octopus spends its life creeping about the rocks and holes of the ocean floor. Although it is the largest octopus in the world, the Pacific variety shares much in common with others in its family. Each of its eight legs is equipped with two rows of suckers. The legs are attached to a saclike body. The body has a strange beaked mouth and a well-developed brain. The Pacific octopus attacks only moving objects, gliding toward its victim, then jumping with a sudden backward spurt to trap the prey beneath the web of its body. If alarmed, the octopus can release a cloud of ink.

The octopus is one of the most adept animals at camouflaging itself. It may appear dark or dull white or display a swiftly changing pattern of colors. Octopus saliva contains a nerve poison that paralyzes small prey and can even be dangerous or fatal to humans. When mating, the only contact between the male and female is through a single arm that the male extends to fertilize the female. Within a week the female lays about 150,000 eggs, each in a capsule the size of a grain of rice. The mother incubates the eggs for several weeks, cleaning them with her arms or blowing water over them. The newly hatched octopuses are about $\frac{1}{8}$ inch long. They drift about until they are four times bigger—large enough to begin their lives on the ocean floor.

Orangutan
Pongo pygmaeus

Length: 31 to 38 inches
Height (sitting): 2¼ to 3 feet
Weight: 88 to 200 pounds
Diet: fruits and plant shoots

Number of Young: 1
Home: Sumatra and Borneo
Order: primates
Family: great apes

  Rain Forests

Mammals

© D. ROBERT & LORRI FRANZ / CORBIS

? Endangered Animals

Orangutans are large, shy apes. They move easily through the trees. They use their arms to swing from branch to branch. Their arms are very long. When an orangutan stands up, its arms can touch its ankles. The orangutan can climb very high. It can reach the top of the highest tree. On the ground, it nearly always moves on all fours. It is not like the chimpanzee, which usually walks on its hind legs.

Orangutans live a solitary life. But sometimes an orangutan couple can be seen with their young. They feed on fruits. They especially like wild figs. The orangutan makes a nest out of leaves each evening. The nest looks like a soft platform. It is often placed in a tall tree. The orangutan protects itself from rain and sun by putting large leaves on its head. Sometimes it winds leaves completely around its head and neck. Orangutans are the most silent of all apes. They grunt and smack their lips once in a while. Occasionally, an orangutan makes a sound like a lion's roar. It may roar to tell other apes of its group where it is. If it is disturbed by humans, it shakes branches. It makes all the noise it can.

Orangutans live in the tropical forests of Sumatra and Borneo. They are becoming very rare. They once were found in China and Java. They are endangered by illegal hunting. They are sometimes captured for zoos and circuses. This also threatens their survival.

Golden Oriole
Oriolus oriolus

Length: about 10 inches
Weight: about 2¾ ounces
Diet: insects and fruits
Number of Eggs: 3 or 4
Home: *Summer:* Europe
  Winter: tropical Africa and India

Order: perching birds
Family: crows, jays

Forests and Mountains

Birds

☐ Summer ■ Winter

© JORGE SIERRA / OSF / ANIMALS ANIMALS / EARTH SCENES

Of the 28 species of oriole, the male golden oriole of Europe is unmistakable. It is dressed in brilliant yellow with black wing and tail feathers. The dull yellowish green feathers of the females and young are not nearly as showy.

In spring, golden orioles fly north from the African tropics. As the flocks pass across Europe, mated pairs settle in woodlands and orchards to breed and raise their young. Despite the male's bright colors, golden orioles are more often heard than seen. They rarely come to the ground. They prefer to stay in the highest, thickest treetops. From their hidden perches, the birds sing a beautiful flutelike song. "Weela-weeo," they warble, again and again.

The male golden oriole is a lively suitor. He chases the female through the treetops at breakneck speed. As he does, he sweeps over and under the branches. After mating, the female does most of the nest building. First she weaves a deep, cup-shaped nest. She then hangs it like a sock between the forks of a branch. Her eggs are white or light pink with many rich, dark spots. Both parents take turns warming the eggs and feeding the chicks. The entire task—from egg laying to teaching the chicks to fly—takes no more than a month. However, the young birds often stay with their parents until it is time to fly south in the fall.

Arabian Oryx
Oryx leucoryx

Length: 5⅓ feet
Height: 3 feet
Weight: 140 to 155 pounds
Diet: grasses, herbs, and roots
Number of Young: 1
Home: Saudi Arabia and Oman

Order: even-toed hoofed mammals
Family: antelope, bison, buffalo, cattle, goats, and sheep

 Deserts

 Mammals

© STEVE KAUFMAN / CORBIS

Endangered Animals

Life has never been easy for the Arabian oryx. This large antelope is also known as the white oryx. It has always lived in the barren steppes and deserts of Saudi Arabia and the Near East. There it must survive without water for days at a time. It is also forced to live on a diet of tough herbs and grasses. The Arabian oryx's natural enemies once included jackals, lions, leopards, and cheetahs. All but the jackal have been driven from Arabia. Unfortunately, game hunters are responsible for the decline in the animals' populations.

People chased the oryx in cars and even planes. Thus they slaughtered entire herds in a single day. By 1965 only a few Arabian oryx remained. So scientists captured some and brought them to the Phoenix Zoo in Arizona. This small zoo herd has been successful. About a dozen offspring from the group have been returned to Oman. The country's ruling sultan protects them. Still, there may be fewer than 100 Arabian oryx in the world today.

Both male and female Arabian oryx have dramatic saberlike horns. They grow up to 2¼ feet long. The males use their sabers to do battle. But they do not spear their opponents. (This could prove deadly.) Rather, oryx "fence" with each other; that is, the males exchange blows with the long sides of their horns. Only in times of drought have oryx been known to stab each other. Their deadly fights are usually over a water hole.

Osprey
Pandion haliaetus

Height: 21 to 24 inches
Wingspan: 54 to 72 inches
Diet: fish, rodents,
   crustaceans, and small
   vertebrates

Number of Eggs: 2 to 4
Home: worldwide
Order: daytime birds of prey
Family: eagles, hawks

 Freshwater

 Birds

The osprey is a brown, gull-like hawk. It lives along the seacoast and near large rivers. The osprey can rotate its outer toe completely to the rear. This adaptation helps the bird capture fish, its principal prey. An osprey out looking for its next meal hovers high above the surface of the water. When it spots its prey, the bird swoops down from the sky feet first. It grabs its victim with its long, curved talons. After feeding, the osprey apparently "washes" its feet by dragging them through the water while flapping its wings.

Osprey nests are large, bulky affairs. They are often 6 feet across. And they're composed of randomly arranged sticks, sod, and seaweed. After mating, the female is fed entirely by the male until she lays her eggs.

Both parents incubate the two to four boldly marked eggs. The eggs hatch in about five weeks. The downy young are fed exclusively by the mother with food brought to the nest by the father. The young ospreys remain in the nest for about 60 days.

Although not officially endangered, ospreys are considered rare. Their populations suffered severely from exposure to the now banned pesticide DDT. They were also affected by hunting and the commercial development of their breeding grounds. Their numbers have increased somewhat with the DDT ban. And conservation programs utilizing artificial nesting platforms have also helped their population grow. Ospreys are one of the few birds of prey found on every continent.

Ostrich
Struthio camelus

Height: 8 feet
Weight: 150 to 250 pounds
Diet: plant shoots, leaves, flowers, seeds, and some small animals
Number of Eggs: 4 to 8

Home: Africa south of the Sahara
Order: cassowaires, emus, and relatives
Family: ostriches

 Grasslands

 Birds

© PAUL VAN GAALEN / ZEFA / CORBIS

Endangered Animals

A strange bird can sometimes be seen in the African savanna. It has long, powerful legs. But it cannot fly because its wings are too tiny. It runs when in danger. This bird is the ostrich. It runs on its toes. It is the only bird that has two toes on each foot. Ostriches can run faster than almost any animal. The only one faster is the cheetah.

Ostriches are very tall. They can stand as tall as 8 feet. They are also very strong. But they are afraid of people. So their habits are not well known. Ostriches mainly eat plants. They like to eat roots and seeds. Like many birds, they swallow stones. The stones help break up food in their gizzards.

At mating time, the males fight for the females. They peck, kick, and hiss. Females share nests. Two to five females will all lay their eggs in one nest. The nest can hold up to 60 eggs! The male ostrich sits on them most of the time. The huge eggs weigh more than 3 pounds each. They can resist the weight of the 240-plus-pound male ostrich.

The ostrich was once hunted for its beautiful feathers. The large bird almost totally disappeared. One type, the Arabian ostrich, became extinct. Strict rules were necessary to save the African ostriches from extinction.

Canadian Otter
Lontra canadensis

Length: 20 to 40 inches
Length of Tail: 12 to 20 inches
Weight: 10 to 30 pounds
Diet: fish, other mammals, and water birds
Number of Young: 1 to 4

Home: Canada and the United States
Order: carnivores
Family: badgers, otters, skunks, weasels, and relatives

 Freshwater

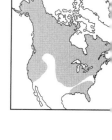

Mammals

© JOE MCDONALD / CORBIS

The Canadian otter is a playful creature found in Canada (especially along the coast of British Columbia), Alaska, and the southern part of the United States. It has a sleek body with a rounded head, short legs, webbed feet, and strong claws. Its fine, dark brown fur is nearly waterproof. Like other river otters, it is known for its long, muscular, and flexible tail, which is an efficient propeller in the water.

The Canadian otter usually makes its den in the bank of a waterway or in a hollow log. Its diet is primarily fish, but the otter is also known to eat mammals such as muskrat and beaver, as well as various water birds. Canadian otters mate in spring, just after the birth of a litter. Females bear their young between April and June. Usually one to four kittens are born at a time; the female cares for their young until the next litter is due. It takes two years for the kittens to mature.

Canadian otters are known to hunt alone at night, especially if the moon is shining. They are excellent swimmers and divers, and can stay underwater for six to eight minutes before coming up for air. Otters seem to enjoy swimming on their backs or sides. When food is scarce, otters travel great distances, sometimes crossing mountain ranges. Excessive trapping has decreased their numbers, and air and water pollution have also taken a toll on this gentle species.

Sea Otter
Enhydra lutris

Length: 3 to 4 feet
Weight: 50 to 100 pounds (male); 30 to 70 pounds (female)
Diet: shellfish, crabs, sea urchins, fish, and seaweed
Number of Young: 1

Home: coasts of Alaska, California, and the Aleutian Islands
Order: carnivores
Family: badgers, otters, skunks, weasels, and relatives

 Oceans and Shores

Mammals

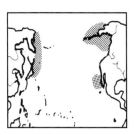

? Endangered Animals

© KENNAN WARD / CORBIS

The sea otter is an excellent swimmer. It has a sleek, round body and a short tail. It has webbed rear feet. The sea otter loves the water. It seldom visits land. It eats, mates, and gives birth at sea. At dusk, the sea otter falls asleep on the water, wrapped in seaweed.

A sea otter dives to look for food. It may dive as deep as 130 feet. It uses its feet to grab food. It can quickly catch a crab, a mussel, or a sea urchin. Then the otter brings it back to the surface. It swims on its back, so it can use its stomach as a table while it eats! It is the only meat eater known to use a tool. The sea otter breaks shells by using a stone. It picks up stones from the bottom of the ocean. It is always cleaning and smoothing its fur. So the fur is shiny and thick. The fur holds air that keeps the sea otter warm. This clean and fluffy fur is like a blanket. If the fur gets dirty, the otter might die from the cold. People once paid a lot of money for sea otter fur. Sea otters were overhunted. Many were killed in the early 1900s. But now the sea otter is protected. So its numbers have increased.

The sea otter can have young at any time of the year. Mating takes place about every two years. The young otter is born in the water. It begins to dive when it's two months old. But it stays near its mother for six to eight months. The mother swims on her back and carries the baby on her stomach.

Barn Owl
Tyto alba

Length: 14 to 20 inches
Wingspan: 12¼ inches to 14 inches
Weight: 15½ to 17 ounces
Diet: rodents and other small animals

Number of Eggs: 5 to 7
Home: North America, South America, Africa, Australia, Europe, and Asia
Order: goatsuckers, owls
Family: barn-owls

 Cities, Towns, and Farms

 Birds

© MAURICE WALKER / FRANK LANE PICTURE AGENCY / CORBIS

The barn owl does not hunt in forests. In this way it is unlike its relatives. It swoops down on its prey in open fields, meadows, and marshes. It's easy to see why this owl often lives in barns. From a tall farm building, a barn owl can look out over the field. It will find plenty of mice and other little animals. Unfortunately, the number of barn owls in North America is getting smaller. So is the number of small family farms.

Some birds communicate with one another by their position. Others use their brightly colored feathers. But barn owls and their relatives communicate almost entirely by sound. This is because owls are active at night. And it is hard to see at that time of day. Barn owls have at least 15 different calls. The one sound they never make is the "hoot-hoot" of other owls. Instead, they hiss, purr, and snore. Barn owls also communicate in other ways. They click their tongues and clap their wings. But their most familiar sound is a long, strange screech. The males use this scary sound to claim their territory. What else does this sound do? It scares off other males and attracts females.

Male and female pairs stay together for several years. Sometimes they are together for life. They are very loving parents. Together, they care for their young for almost two months. It takes this long for the chicks to learn to fly and hunt.

Boreal Owl
Aegolius funereus

Length: 9 to 10 inches
Diet: mainly rodents and small birds
Number of Eggs: 3 to 6

Home: Canada, Europe, and Asia
Order: goatsuckers, owls
Family: typical owls

Forests and Mountains

Birds

© MARCELLO CALANDRINI / CORBIS

The boreal owl's soft face feathers form a round disk that gives the bird a look of constant surprise. Adding to its dramatic expression are the owl's piercing yellow eyes. The boreal owl's call is a light, repeated note that sounds somewhat like dripping water or a small bell.

The boreal owl is able to survive, even thrive, in the cold northern forests. In summer the woods teem with prey, such as mice and birds. But the owl's food virtually disappears in the fall, when many small animals hibernate or migrate south. Usually active only at night, the boreal owl must hunt around the clock to find enough to eat in winter. This is not as strange for the owl as you might imagine. In the far north,

darkness lasts 24 hours a day for much of December, January, and February.

In spring the male boreal owl calls from the top of a spruce or other tall coniferous tree. When a female approaches, the courting male leads her to his chosen nest hole. He then presents her with a gift of food. This can be a recently killed mouse, which he has stored there. The male continues to serenade his mate until she moves into his nest and lays her eggs.

Many owl species hide from people. But the boreal owl acts surprisingly tame. In Europe this species is called Tengmalm's owl. There it gladly moves into human-made nest boxes when tree holes are not available.

Great Horned Owl
Bubo virginianus

Length: 18 to 24 inches
Diet: mammals, birds, reptiles, and insects
Number of Eggs: 2 to 3

Home: North and South America
Order: goatsuckers, owls
Family: typical owls

 Forests and Mountains

 Birds

© JOE MCDONALD / CORBIS

The great horned owl ranks among the largest and strongest of the world's owls. It gets its name from the horn-shaped tufts of feathers on top of its head. While most birds are active during the day, the great horned owl spends the night away from its nest, or roost. The great horned owl is a superb nighttime hunter. Its big, wide eyes gather the dim light, and its powerful legs and talons help it catch and kill prey. Despite being such a formidable predator, the owl can sometimes be intimidated by its prey. In a type of behavior called "mobbing," two or more small birds will fly around an owl to warn others and try to chase the owl away.

The very adaptable great horned owl usually makes a home in an old nest of another large bird or in the hollow of a tree or a rocky crevice. Sometimes it digs its own nest in the ground. In North America, horned owls begin breeding in winter and lay their eggs from January to April. Most remain in the same area throughout their lives, although some groups in the far north migrate to escape the harsh winter.

The familiar "hoo-hoo-hoo" sound that we associate with owls belongs only to this species. Other owls have quite different calls. The female horned owl has a lower-pitched voice than the male. When both sing together, their voices blend in beautiful harmony.